DIME SAINT, NICKEL DEVIL

Also by Ann Lauinger

Persuasions of Fall
Against Butterflies

DIME SAINT, NICKEL DEVIL

ANN LAUINGER

Poems

For Chris —

Such a pleasure to meet you — fellow poet & fellow Sarah Lawrentian!

Ann

Broadstone

Broadstone Books
An Imprint of
Broadstone Media LLC
418 Ann Street
Frankfort, KY 40601-1929
BroadstoneBooks.com

for Joe
always, all ways

CONTENTS

Part Three

PART ONE

Girl Reading the *Aeneid* on the Subway

What she makes of all that myth and destiny
Is anybody's guess. Other towers
For other times. Of course it's also ours,
The ten-years' war, but she's too young for history.

Poor Aeneas, predestined to succeed
And mean to Dido, gets no sympathy
From most her age. Yet, brushing absently
Her pale hair from light eyes, she seems to read

Intently, concentrating from her perch,
A sunlit bird oblivious to this grotto
Of sibylline scraps, of ear-buds' rhythmic *sotto*
Voce boom, of medicated lurch.

What's at our backs, the weight by which we're driven,
Unhinges us—the great ones more than most,
Who know, though desert-bleached and tempest-tossed,
That to be great is not to be forgiven.

Not that it's safer or saner to be small.
Look at us, jolted down tracks in loveless tandem,
The endless ride to inquietude, our random
Days without distinction, nights in free-fall.

She rises, marks her place with a neat, white square
And zips in her bag the journeys and the wars.
I glimpse her rising still beyond shut doors,
Fate dangling from a strap, to meet the upper air.

Two Ravens

Two ravens pause at two nodes,
self-engrossed. Two bents

of mind, two overlapping
maps of myriad unseen lines.

Pale sky implies a sea as vast,
past pulse, the future ghost.

In this disquietude we can rest.
All signs suggest the claims

they press on us are equal, what
we see and what we never will.

Dime Saint, Nickel Devil

It takes a certain talent for bewilderment
to be a saint; that's why they're not a dime
a dozen. Wondering takes up all their time.
They wonder themselves to sleep, they wonder
stumbling out to pee. They chew their coarse
bread in wonder, wonder their voices hoarse
with prayer, wander wondering until they drop,
then do it all again because it doesn't
make sense, and that's called God.

I've been bewildered, but I've only ever pondered—
wonder's cousin from the airless tenements.
Mine fits snugly, the bespoke bewilderment
of a May afternoon cut just to my measure.
Or so the silent chime of nodding bells avers
and sky the color of grace and ministering birds.
The draught is equal parts petals scattered
at a wedding and oblivion like a memory of lilacs.
I'm fated to surrender to pure sense.

The next day the deer have come and dined.
In that angry winter, desires were grubs,
graceful branches browsed right down to stubs.
Pondering means weighing, but what against what?
The euonymus did leaf again, glossy and rife.
When the young man's heart stopped, his doctor-wife
couldn't start it. Art Tatum jams "Deep Purple"
like a homecoming march. How can elegy become energy?
If it isn't nonsense, the devil must be in it.

Persimmons on the Ground

In a world of so much ruined beauty, look
      here. Palace lights fallen, split
            and smashed on the ground. Brilliance

down. Oh, it's a sadist's dream! Gelatinous,
      satiny flesh there for the scooping,
            skin peeled in broad horizontal,

skin fringed as if by the haircutter's shears.
      Each luminous wreck of skin and flesh
            still wears its crown, a star

of brown leaves. Why should you imagine fat
      sad clowns in torn costumes
            and too-small hats? (The tents

are down, the circus train has departed.) Look here
      at decomposition. Speak,
            if you speak, of fallen brilliance. Flesh and stars.

PRINCIPLES

I'm in favor of them, generally. Here's one:
    The Systematic Squashing Effect of Ordinary Life,

which explains the way one flattening leads to another.
    So, thanks to our well-meaning sanitation workers,

the old zinc garbage lid, dinged and flattened in the street,
    has now flattened its own dead zone on the hedge.

But it doesn't explain how, the thousandth time I grabbed
    that lid, the dead zone boiled and writhed with life.

What could have been a sloppy coil of tarred rope
    or discarded bicycle tires in a striped and knotted heap—

but for three obsidian chips, three lidless eyes—
    snapped into sudden view as looped and intertwining

yards and yards of snake-flesh that just as suddenly seethed
    apart and was gone. Systematic Squashing didn't cover

this one: a new principle seemed in order, but what?
    Quick clicking gave me "A breeding ball" and "The mating season

of the Eastern garter snake is March to May." This being September,
    maybe it's Climate Change Screws with Snakes Screwing.

Or Plan Nine from Outer Space. On second thought,
    to hell with principles. And to hell with names.

I won't presume to explain a shocking grace. Or guess
    what may, or may not, come to bless the place.

Imago

is the word for the adult butterfly that emerges from
    its chrysalis, but since I will probably never
        witness this singular and defining
            moment of a creature so
                unlike me,
            I wish I'd been riding
        the jolting, arrhythmic bus that took
    Lucy home those Saturdays from her paper-
making apprenticeship, because then I could have seen

for myself her accidental cocoon and how, with single-
    minded absorption, she unwound pulpy strips
        like bandages from arms, palms, and
            fingertips, a task timed for
                completion
            just as the bus reached her
        stop, when the double doors folded back
    like wings and Lucy stepped into all her futures
from that dry scattering of scraps, the puzzle of an image.

ALL SAINTS' EVE AT THE DRUNKEN CACTUS

What is the timid stripper thinking while she works?
       She twirls the telescope of her cowardice at both ends,
ashamed of her tame heart. Enlarged and near

are the babies, bellies on sticks, women carved
       and blinded. The shadow of a praying mantis
on a white fence is distant, minute and clear,

a thin and sour grace: herself abridged.
       Disfigurements burn her eyes: a sprawl of blackened
vines, pocked rinds collapsing, faces melted,

torsos hacked….Like twin altars, pleasure
       and agony tower in gold and polished bones.
She doesn't know how to dig, she can't climb.

She longs to be generous. Like a spider throwing its silk?
       (That's not it.) She struggles to give thanks
to no one. By the time she gets off work,

the rising wind will have swept the night sky
       into cloudy prognostications. Plastic shards
of sticky red will testify to the vanished

mob of vampires, the zombie-women trailing
       black synthetic tresses, the green-skinned
ghouls, all haunting the subway, un-dead

on their feet. At the dark bar, Pirate Cactus Jack
       leers and glows. She lets the pole slide
through clasped thighs, walks off and thinks,

Doesn't my heart flame too? She's flesh, not chitin-
       clad; her hands are warm and meant to grasp
someone's, not steel. But the street's all hers. Only

a few stars, steady sailors' marks, are watching
    fantastic drifts of cloud, like dolphins, mass
and thin. Their teasing shapes at play unveil

and cloak, then half-reveal again—what?
    Something, cold and sudden, hums across
her blood, seizing her with spaniel care.

Bridegroom, wed me to your flood, your air.
    For all the saints' sake, strengthen my loneliness
to bear it—most of all, what is not there.

Heat Wave

Late summer noon
comes booming between two blues,
doubled light shaking down heat
from its metaled globe like snow.
An eddy of last year's leaves
signals some gliding flash-haunt.
Only the phlox and hydrangea—
blue, cotton candy, magenta—
stir motion in difference,
almost a tune.
I want to yell, but this torrent
of light stoppers my breath.
I'm a torn moth, mute,
blot on the page
of a book slammed shut.
Future ghost.

The Parlor Wit

She organized her disappointments
like earrings, in a smart case
of rosewood and velvet-lined compartments.
The trick was shrinkage.

Having felt (once) the prick of compassion,
intent, she fingered the scab like Braille
and tried to imagine the look of a lashing
and wanted to fail.

A parlor wit of passing flashes
and gibes, gilt-winged ephemerid.
By nightfall, ash among the ashes,
stridulous, exhausted.

Tip-tailed wren, whose dizzy trill,
silken and compulsive quaver
bespangled the littleness so well
we almost forgave her

diaphanous life, all corner and keyhole,
carious, rank. How fervent my hope
she'd jump and trust to her parasol:
I was a dope.

A moral miniaturist, keen to trace
with finely graded camel-hair brushes
anything inconsequential, her gaze
was averted always—

even at the mirror, fixed on the frame.
Is there damnation by inches? Unfit
as she was for either frost or flame,
I guess this was it.

CONTRADANCE

Would you catch a snake
In a noose of silk?
Tame a tiger
To drink your milk?

Green as sorrow,
Gold as good:
I thought by now
I'd have understood.

In the ticklish grass
What sidewise sighs?
If-Only's rumpled
Skirts flash by.

Rearview looms small,
Not yours to keep.
Ahead lies Never,
Too broad to leap.

Penny for the ferryman,
Penny for a chance,
Penny for the fiddler
To make you all dance.

Sashay, shoofly,
Up to town and back.
Hoof it, clog it, stomp it
Till the stars burn black.

DOLLY GETS OLDER

Proofs?

One, the kitten is a cat now and sleeps all day.
Two, the begonia drops all its red stars,
every stalk bows to the ground.

So.

(That's how the man across the desk begins,
who keeps your files and lab reports and knows
the things you hope you never have to know.)
Let's look at your options, shall we?

No!

She does not want to land on Three.
Time has no feel, no smell.
But she can see its great steam-shovel claw of steel,
tireless and indestructible. And it can
go to hell.

Proverbs for Complicated Times

Two birds in the cage have more fun than one in the hand. And it doesn't hurt if the cage is gilded.

Ask me no questions and I'll tell you what happens in Vegas stays out of mind but makes the heart grow fonder.

Keeping everlastingly at it brings numbness.

Sticks and stones may break my bones, but names will initiate lengthy and punitively expensive legal proceedings.

Babies who live in glass houses shouldn't throw out their bath water.

It takes two wrongs to tango right.

Early to bed, early to rise, and the wise child catches its own father turning into a worm.

Haste not—want not—nothing gained.

POEMS ABOUT POETRY

I, too, dislike them, my own included. They remind me of a muddy pigeon's preening—a glancing iridescence, but on the whole a laborious process of more utility and pleasure to the agent than anyone else.

In the gardens of the Alhambra, shadow traceries fall from fretworks that resist a remorseless sun. In their making, the hard rock opposed every hammer-blow, flake by flake.

And my imaginary gardens? They're too easily planned and planted. How flattering their dazzlements of design, how eagerly their frilled brilliance and lush spiralings respond to my whims.

There's more resistance in eating an apple or learning to play the ocarina. I should seriously study toads, their shining, un-saccadic gaze, their croaking chorus, which might

with luck become a roar then grow into a cataract tumbling me (anxious paddler) ass over teakettle, my only chance now to flail away toward the strange, the worded shore.

Was It Bashō

who regretted that
his mind was sometimes
a leaky bucket

sometimes hummingbird-
glitter frantic in
its bamboo cage: too

empty or too full?

THE MATCH

in memory of Kim Bridgford

"The trouble is the body,"
she wrote, with a clang like

a midway bell hammered just
right. She had that knack.

I began to think (as if
her smarts and sense could

be contagious) I might write
back: "Kim, isn't it the mind?"

I sketched a thought, something
about the body's portals to

sensation's riches, something else
about how the mind can

piss on any party. What then?
This wasn't tennis. Opposites

make the toughest, the most
necessary pairs, but sooner

or later, whether yoked by love,
chance or need, uncouple, fail

each other: Laurel and Hardy,
Antony and Cleopatra, Mind

and Body. I want to say: Kim,
call it spirit or matter, a stubborn

something lives still. As complex
harmony rearranges air, or night

traces the Geminids' disappearing flare.
As breath's and body's children—

words—buckle the wide
silence of their breeding

into something uttered,
something heard.

CRADLE

Picture each joint of the body
a sailor's hammock of tendons
and ligaments, the habit of motion

secured to a rope cradle
sea-tilted, swinging in air.
Even forgotten, the body reminds

itself of itself. Repose
finds poses: cheek in hand,
ankles crossed, knee-cap

in fossa resting, nested
like cups. But think of the body's
weft unpicked from warp,

shuttle stilled, stopper knots
slipped, sheet bends slackened.
Would I sail free?

Most likely, unmoored
only means bereft, an end
to rockabye, Daedalus helpless

at the death of metaphor,
his grasp outstretched between
grievances of sea and sky.

Scene, with Supporting Cast of Facts

The Wren's flown off, trailing the thread
of my discontent in her beak. She

has a use for it. I don't. Here are
the two Tall Oaks: one fallen in last night's

storm, the robust other not fallen
yet. These are facts, but hard for me to

learn the use of. Four, no five Deer stepped
to the stream, then leapt it. All creatures

step to the stream in their time, which is
not my time. This may be justice, a curve

so vast I'll call it imperceptible, but
strict too, demanding for fulfillment

my end in something not-me. Last
of all, the Rainbow Stand-In,

darling of all screens, its specious
wholeness lying and falsifying, only

its fading sheen more useful, beautiful,
and true than what I wish, what I wish to mean.

White Bird / Bare Tree

An egret, or maybe a heron.
This bird-app's terrible: I need
a better guide. Look at the bird,
how calmly prodigal. It would be a shame
to waste the light it throws.
In its candid plumage,
the stripped boughs are leafed again.

Let Me Knot

Let me not to the marriage of true minds
Admit impediments.

To test our desolation, I rose from dark to dark.

Peaks of glassy basalt, the local stone, strode silent.
I ascended by careful enumeration,
inscribing the day's black blazon:

>   charred hemlock trunks, cinder tracks,
>   burnt thatch, dark windows, dead hearth.

The air grew thinner and so did I.

I emptied my packs and pockets
yet felt my footfall less free,
a born stumbler, foot-dragging
my natural form of locomotion.

Just within sight of my goal, the lake so hidden
they say it never reflects blue sky,
I twisted my quit-song, that mortal coil.

Forced into bloom, a red tulip lurched in my chest.
Oh brave mountaineer!
Now I'm no more than my boot tips kicking the scree,
tied by the heartstrings to all my loved impediments.

The Difference

Whether I heard or saw it first is moot,
a rustling arched toward a gap in the porch roof.
An inquiring beak, the curve's continuation,
gave a prod too brief to complete its investigation
of a niche to build a nest. Retire, rest,
repeat. One common sparrow's furious quest,
compulsion of the ordinary, fevered desire
focused, simple, noble (I thought) as fire—
and my phrases rose like a flock of birds
dispersed, driven to make a home of words.
That sparrow had the right stuff; I envied its sense
of purpose. A common error: its incandescence
shone with *purpose*, but *sense*? It was only me
who tethered the two. The one with feathers flew free.

ABOUT THE PONIES
after W.H. Auden

About the ponies they were always wrong,
the old bastards down at Bruegel's bar,
but I kept waiting for a miracle and standing them beers.
I figured it couldn't be all baloney, they'd been around so long.
Sal with his poker-table
tips he gets from a guy whose sister's kid
can't hold a job and hangs around the course,
so sometimes they let him hose down a stable.
And now it's Bow-Tie's got this problem with his ear,
and it's making him dizzy, and that means the horse
is gonna scratch. Then Frank
gets all excited, says Licorice is in the clear
now the rabbit's out, it's money in the bank,
Ripcord's a closer, no way he wins—
it don't matter if he's three-to-two—
believe me, right now (he says) where we stand,
we got better odds of seeing that horse *and*
his rider do a slow fall out of the blue.

The Amaryllis

"Not guaranteed to bloom a second year"
means "Don't complain." But see the ambiguity?
Not "Guaranteed *not* to bloom": that would be clear.
You would have tended to it just like me:
watered it, sunned it, checked for pests and disease,
and brought it inside well before its leaves,
long drooping spears, got nipped by autumn freeze.

The anniversary of its splendor came
and went. I watered faithfully, I fed,
without a hope of blooms. The only claim
it had on me was memory—the red,
wide-mouthed clangor of its bells last year,
and weather mean enough to make a friend
of anything that chanced to be in here.

I grew to think of it as a great-aunt
subsisting on sweetened tea in my spare room,
all but forgotten—no trouble, but someone you can't
evict. In May, a bulge I dared not assume
would bud shot up, parting its oval case.
Some grief relaxed its spiky jaws and fled,
unlooked-for scarlet giving brilliant chase.

PART TWO

TYRANNY (I)

Tell me why marriage, once upon a time,
entailed such a legion of silver things to eat with.
Like this olive spork, with two devil's-horn
prongs and a bottomless bowl: you get to choose
whether to cradle your snack or stab it. I own three
olive sporks—plus a caseful of other weird
and needless tools for eating-as-display.
Had the Prince Regent ever stopped for lunch
in the Bronx, my grandmother was ready. Today,
laid on my chipped tile counter while I pull on
rubber gloves, the whole array fails utterly
to conjure lobster tart, or doves in aspic,
and only makes me think of tonsillectomies.
But I'm caught. I polish the stuff, just never enough
to keep the tarnish and black spots at bay. Dump it,
sell it, get amnesia? Give it away
to some relative I detest? Impossible.
How did I get to this intersection of Beauty
and Duty, rubbing pink paste into filigree?
I've read about tears in things.
There's tyranny too, although they
didn't think so, who (before vanishing) shined
these fish forks and cheese knives, showed off the cake slices,
demitasse spoons, and handed me down silver
pieces as though they were tickets from memory's pawn shop,
pledges (no matter how hard I polish) of love
that none I loved can ever return to redeem.

Sunrise (Prime)

Sunrise reboots the laptop. Ambushed again.
A pack of leash-jingling vehicles
snuffles and waits for their tenors to kick in.
I never asked for a virgin world:
when I was a child, a plump new pad,
a pristine tray of paints made me cry.
The only picture conceivable
to my proleptic eyes
was of sad, scraped hollows
in their wasted tin, awash in white
crumpled billows of dissatisfaction.
No surprise if I prefer the dawn second-hand,
reflected on the western hills. Better still
is waking to motors already humming
in pre-owned *medias res*.
I love this world too well to stamp it mine—
so well, a sunrise nearly stops my heart
when I see how cunningly the end
disguises itself as a fresh start.

BACKYARD (TIERCE)

Hail connubial earth! Hail wedded commerce
of all that shoot, suck, creep in fruitful promise!

There was no verb but be in Paradise;
now, the shovel jars and grinds. He pries

up rocks, tosses them at the woman's feet.
They've been assured their small garden has great

potential, meaning patchy and overgrown.
So far its most abundant crop is stone—

and a hand-picked harvest of early-ripe quarrels.
The holes where bulbs were dug up by the squirrels,

the dropped leaves of mildewed roses, sparseness
of the peony blooms are signs to her no less

clear than the doom spelled on Belshazzar's wall.
Nothing will flourish for her. She's The Fatal

Gardener, whose careful fostering always deprives
her charges of the will to live. Nothing thrives.

The man is digging where he thinks, with luck,
there may be fewer stones. Hairy and thick,

roots (of what old menace?) resist his tugging.
Pulled taut and clipped, they're even uglier

than at first look. Is that his rotator cuff
or something worse? And is it work or love

that sweats into the dirt of this bright June?
They won't figure that out anytime soon.

Baby Mantis ·

elegant little horror

     all elbow and wrist

cunning jeweled hatchling

     half-inch filament-twist

paper clip inflexion

     flanged pulse at rest

transparently illegible

     bride/mate/feast

PROFIT

Not one of those splashy bloomers
I envied on other people's lawns,
yet, hemmed in between house
and hedge, the magnolia
flowers each May, and I count
the buds, repeatedly
which means obsessively.
I bet I could give each one a name
like Jane Goodall's chimps
except I'm nothing like Jane Goodall,
more like some wooden, sad
old miser out of Balzac.
I count the pink blazing flowers too:
It feels like profit.

So where was the satisfaction
when the end of summer brought
an extra dividend, a second flowering?
Everywhere, the viral florescence
was bringing us to our knees. I was
swimming in all kinds of red ink,
ready to close the books
on summer, till this fresh crop
of fiery petals rained
down on my neatly ruled columns
like starlight from a far treasury where
place means time and radiance leaping from *was*
to *will be* replenishes *now*, the casual
happiness that can't be saved or spent.

Noon (Sext)

Give me some light! cried Claudius.
Me too, I said, easily seduced
by full disclosure in the market square.
That hot noon gaze! The years I spent
flaunting my tan and combing news
out of the ozone-freighted air.

How did we stand the monkey-chatter,
blinded, stewing, in the bald glare?
Noon's such a boring palindrome.
But clock-hands have the right idea,
and in our private hemisphere
it's midnight. Darling, let's go home.

THE CRIMSON HYPOTHESIS

See with what simplicity
This Nimph begins her golden daies!

Andrew Marvell, "The Picture of little T.C. in a Prospect of Flowers"

I know I am to meditate on Beautie
When I see it, not to gawp at it like
Mad Agnes the Almswoman
Before the kitchen Fire, and especially not
To covet what I see. Looking
Is a great Sinne if it be covetously done.
I have watch'd the Amaryllis every Day in Advent.
As the Days grow shorter, two green Stalks
Shoot taller from the dirt. I am thinking
About this. The scarser the Day-light becomes,
The more Avid for it are the growing Shoots.
I am also thinking, Something green in me
Works, by Gods Grace, toward the Light.
The Stalks bud, and redden, and open, four
Crimson Flowers upon each; they are Bells
As big as my fist. I am thinking about these too,
How the Rod of Jesse flower'd in the Years mid-Night;
Though the Revd. Mr. Starkey has never said
What Color the Flowers were, nor what Kind.
I am trying to think about how each Stalk bears
Four Blossoms, as it were Points of the Compass,
Or, it might be better to think, they make
A crimson Cross. I know the Cross of our Redemption
Flower'd with the Blood of our Lord, and I am thinking
About that. But Blood is not trewlie this Color of red.
And, is it proper moreover, to apply such a weightie
Likeness to the Flowers, their Petals being so delicate
And withal so easily crush'd? I begin to fear Meditation
May be a dangerous Busyness. Perhaps I might think
Instead that Amaryllis was among the Gifts carry'd
By the Three Magi to the Manger. (*Amaryllis* looks
Rather like *Myrrhe* when I write them both out.)
It seems to me it would be simpler if I try'd to think

About the Flowers without looking at them.
I know they must fade soon, and drop, and die,
Yet my Meditations must not die with them.
Mr. Starkey says, Improving Thoughts are, as it were
Writ on Bronze, and do Ornament a Mind more becomingly
Than brightest Gems the Body. Then why should I not
Undertake this Experiment, viz., the Meditation
On my Amaryllis with closed Eyes, and my Hypothesis
Shall be that Crimson will burn behind my Eyelids,
Whether open or closed, and Beautie, like the cold
Musick of Bells, stream from my Amaryllis Flowers
In Darknesse and in Light, always and ever.

CHILDREN PLAYING (NONES)

Vidi a lor giochi quivi e a lor canti
ridere una bellezza, che letizia
era ne li occhi a tutti li altri santi.

I saw there at their games and songs
a beauty laughing, which was joy
in the eyes of all the other saints.
Dante, *Paradiso 31*

It must be 3 p.m. in Paradise
when Dante sees the jeweled shore and stream
resolve themselves into the shining Rose
of endlessness, where Mary smiles at games
of sempiternal jump rope, stickball, jacks
which I see kids, who've made good their escape
from slow-rolling prison transport and their six-
hour stretch of cultivation by the state
(so a pimple ball held tightly and released
will reassert itself as a true sphere),
play here where, in a time not pinched or pieced
but, at this Jericho hallelujah hour,
undammed to flow forever as it should,
they know all Dante saw of bliss and good.

NOTRE DAME, APRIL 2019

After the flames, drifting black
flowers, fans, dragons—
sculpted smoke.

We thought the cathedral mourned,
carving new in air
what had burned.

But one dark shape, self-propelled,
streamed, whirled, and never
failed to meld:

swarming the skies, bees,
like praise, rise.

Vespers

Courage comes back with evening.
A bowl of apples.
The bare wood table.
Lamps on, curtains drawn.

The dragons are appeased,
the tilting is over. The bodies
cannot be counted now.

Come inside. Light slips
from your grasp. When the day
is summed, the clear stars
require of you no witness.

THE ALTAR OF THE BEES

In France, bees once did (this is what I read
in a book of miracles) what I want to do:
they built, around the inexpressible Word,

a church inside their hive and made a new
and shivering music, strange bee-chanted hymns.
I want to rise without wings, taste and dance

a language I have only heard in dreams,
syllables nectar-drenched and sweeter silence,
then ferry, pollen-gold up to the hip,

unheard geographies of tongue-delight
home to eyes and mouths in fellowship,
to raise around each brilliant thing becalmed—

the day remembered—traceries of night:
clerestory, portals, milk-and-honied psalms.

THE RELIQUARY

It was not always this way
I can remember not remembering

        rootshove
motion unmoving   leafleafleaf

Stupor then
then remembering

I was
       drawn
           into form.

They sing to me they carry
      me about What I contain

contains me is not birdsounds not rain not
    light hooding and unhooding

What I contain angles
      me hinges me

I remember   I wasn't I
   think   that

is the miracle they sing about.

Progress

Here comes the Royal Harbinger astride his coal-black horse,
his truncheon borne before him and his standard behind.
He is crying up the King's Touch and claiming
"Herborwe, Herborwe!" for the traveling court.
Here come the victualers. They are buying up the mutton, pork,

and poultry, deer, boar, godwits, pheasant, partridge and quail.
They are commandeering orchards, kitchen gardens, and bake ovens.
Here come barrels and barrels roped together like slaves, under
the wary eyes of the butlers, who have been purchasing the beer, sack,
cider, and claret. Here come the cooks and their turnspits, jouncing
on top of wagons where tin and copper pots flame back unbearable

light at the afternoon sun. Here comes the Lord Chamberlain
on his sorrel mount; here is the Master of the Wardrobe with two
dozen leather trunks on the backs of stout lads. Here come the Gentlemen
of the Privy Chamber and those of the Close-stool. Here comes a small
army of carpenters to pitch the tents, unroll the Turkey carpets,

lay down featherbeds on country manor acres a wholesome distance
from the town, which the Chief Steward has politely borrowed
from a dozen vavasours for the night. Here comes the Master of the Hounds
with his beaters, his under-leashers and their thirty couple of baying dogs.
Here come the falconers with their hooded meynie, the tercels, merlins,
and peregrines. The King's Noise follows: sackbuts, cornets, hautboys, viols

like an uprooted forest, liveried in the royal gold and green.
The sun is setting, and still they come. Choristers, boys and men,
a troupe of comedians and one of acrobats. Priests and acolytes,
monks, canons, friars, gowned penitents in white with whips,
a line of brown-robed Holy Sisters of SS. Perpetua and Peripeteia,
chanting the antiphons of the Little Office of Removing. Here comes

the Master of the Horse. The usual urchins, mud-caked and rag-tag,
march mockingly behind the grooms who lead the King's
ten favorite horses, and now the boys break ranks to dodge

among the legs of the slow and brawny armorers who follow.
The dwarf couple gets knocked down in the rush, and the Fool
pulls up each with one hand and dexterously drops both

on the back of a passing horse. Now Night displays her own
celestial progress of banded colors and clouds drifting like smoke
into ink, yet still there is no King. Wait—here comes
a white steed, larger than any of the others, bearing in the saddle
a small boy around whose neck, and so big that it covers the whole
of his slight chest, hangs a black and gold bag stamped with the Royal Arms.

This is the King's personal envoy. Making way for his charger,
the snorting horses jib and rear, a few urchins and a novice are trampled,
the dust as thick as fog foments panic, barrel-laden sledges rock and tip
hazardously, and indeed utter ruin appears imminent, when drums
and cornets sound a flourish, the flourish that means: *Return.*

Ah, but history, like a well-fletched arrow, once released flies
only one way. Return is impossible. Some other direction must
be sought. The Royal Haruspicator and his Under-Skryer consult
in snatches of muttered Greek you can almost see steaming in the air
between their bent, white heads. A pair of wood-doves is released,

then a hawk. A cock's throat is cut and the body whirled three times
overhead and flung away. Full dark has descended.
But the progress slowly re-forms and begins to move, like a giant snake
emerging in early spring from its place of hibernation, spasmodic
bulges and contractions rippling its muscled length. Finding

the road in the dark is not easy nor without incident, but, slowly, orderly
movement resumes. No one mentions dinner or sleep. There is only
the sound of the wagons, the steady clop of the mules and mounts,
and, if you can catch it, a thin, peculiar melody from the hautboys. There goes.

Touch Wood (Compline)

The near-sighted relax at night
thinking, now everybody's just like me,
forced to hazard the known.

Inquiry shines on, but torques its beam
to throw freakish shadows
on the turret walls. It wants to know
who was making all those inquiries
all day long.

Bumping along north of Ulan Bator
on the back of a woolly mammoth,
you've nothing to fear in this dark—
touch wood. Touch fossilized wood
from Ellesmere Island, transformed

by the salts of marine transgression.
Touch ivory that grew in a dream's meander,
spiral tusks like feelers
testing directions: apart, up,
tip toward tip at last. Grip what you can

of those mirror crescent moons.
The mammoth is wading into a cold sea,
making for the far shore.

Matins

Night is still queen over half
the world, too vast to regard
        one small planet

revolving off-kilter,
too velvet-fleshed
        to feel my staccato

hour, the crack of my
disarticulation, myself
        wrenched from myself

at each socket. Ligaments
dissolved, I'm the ghost of a world,
        syntax unstrung,

syllables disjunct, an epigrapher's
fractured and unnumbered clay.
        I'm the sparagmos

of a ruined city, whose flesh still quivers
while something not-flesh cries to be
        locked up again.

Tyranny (II)

So the father of psychoanalysis and the saint
walk into a bar. Not really. But it's funny
how, millennia apart, they're on the same
page about kids. To wit: if children weren't
so small and weak, they'd out-Herod Herod
in envy, lust, and murderous tyranny.
Then what about the boy standing now,
hand on the knob, at his front door? We know
he's old enough to tie his shoes because
he's knotted a handkerchief to hold his plastic
Masters of the Universe action figures
and a slice of bread. Rebel against injustice,
"I'm leaving home," he declares, and does.
What should his mother do: laugh, cry,
panic? The hedge is blocking her view, all
but the bright-brown hair, the same way
her thinking's obscured by love. A minute
passes, two, and there's the hair again,
a home-movie in rewind. The boy flings
himself on her, sobbing, hugging, confessing failure:
"I can't leave home, I love you all too much."
Who's the tyrant here but love? All
we need to know of ruthless domination
we learned from love, his lordship stamped,
scored, burned into us early—and that's
if we're lucky. But, oh, the servitude is golden,
it's cake and silk. And just try to walk free.
No one survives that exile, not even
the ones who haven't a hope of sleep until
they've stripped the sheets from their bed
to knot themselves (by inches) a silken rope.

AUBADE (PRIME)

Up early one summer morning
I raised the blinds to sunstruck
pinks and reds. Cool air
made itself at home. Pleasure
and Virtue stalked their food bowls
in sync. The coffeemaker
expected to be seen to. Done, and done.
And this is happiness, isn't it,
lining up the shining familiar stones?
Or if, at the bottom of Pandora's
Cookie Jar, some sweetness evaded
my fingertips, maybe that was happiness,
and you bearing it downstairs as casually
as you would an empty mug,
the full morning's pennon close-furled,
a magician's nothing-up-your-sleeve you began
to shake out: scarf after knotted
floating scarf, the coming on of love's long day.

THE OLD COUPLE

They've had enough time in this long life
to rehearse the early lesson and get it pat:
things come down to leaving or being left.

What they really crave these days is cats,
the sight of them gravely bathing or sprawled in the sun,
the playful ankle-nipping ambush leap,

their light, reposeful weight on chest or thighs.
As in those 50's films of space invaders
with tapered skulls and vertical-slitted eyes,

cats are emissaries from the fourth dimension.
Their lithe poise of spine from ears to tail
is undisturbed by our awkward, transient lives;

galactic domination rests benignly
in their slender jack-rabbit paws.
Lately both of them dream the same dreams:

embracing, their limbs fuse, hermaphrodite
for good. Cats perch overhead, loll underfoot,
everywhere, and perfectly in command.

No option then but surrender, and so,
creakily folding themselves on hands and knees,
they signal capitulation, The End.

And just like that, The End has ended. Young
and in love, they rise. What rumbling music's this?
May it convoy them wherever their captors will.

PART THREE

INTERROGATORIES

Tell me again what you want.
What will be taken away.

Are you afraid?
Yes.

Tell me about when you were happy.
The lilac leaves shivered at dusk in the garden.

Freud said there is only work and love.
Is that a question?

What are you most afraid of?
Drowning and drought.

Tell me again what you want.
I want beauty.

Would you say the lilac is happy?
It flowers.

Tell me again what you want.
[. . .]

Don't you trust me to help?
As cupping helps a dead man.

Were you afraid in the garden?
No.

What did you dream of last night?
I don't remember.

Did you dream of the garden?
I never dream of the garden.

Tell me again what you want.
Is there nothing but fear and beauty?

American Hallows

You can find the usual suspects at Walgreen's,
but order online and the (Other)world is your oyster.
Mummies, zombies, skeletons.
Cat-skeletons, dragon-skeletons, spider-skeletons (really).
Human skeletons, whole or in pieces.
For the modest who prefer their bones clothed, a pack of mixed body parts.
"Groundbreakers" are big: pose decomposing head and hands
to "rise" from beneath your sod. Add a pop of emerging color with legs
in striped socks, topped with witches' curly-toed shoes.
Once upon a time, we really did believe in once upon a time.
But now, in this bat-shit crazy world, what's a 6-foot clown in a noose
or three pair of—flappable—sable wings? They don't amount to a hill of guano.
Is our imagination that exhausted?
Ugly, sired by Profit out of Plastic, the best we can do
for a night-gallop? No hope then
of catching quick, real fear—living's conjoined twin.

What's that knocking?
I can tell shit from shinola. Shudder me tender, shudder me true.
Accept no cheap substitutes, no greasy kid stuff,
splay me no inflatable nightmares on your lawn.
Better the ghoul you don't know than the ghosts you do.
The real ones sit at your table and feed your fearful murderous heart.
Loss, loss, nothing but loss, sings the children's choir.
Embrace me, beloved, with your phantom limb.

ANGELIC

Wings shading a quattrocento argument
from clavicle to fingertips and thumb.
Drapery fluttering naked flesh.
Mastery of updrafts, hover and pivot
gessoed, rondeled, apsed.

How could we imagine
the new annunciation? Silent plummet,
airborne shock of gold hair streaming.
Supple arms grappling their prey,
our throats bared to the gracile, plunging beak.

The Rest

The common default is a high
closet-shelf, but there are more
choices for ashes. It'll take

arranging, of course, but why not
the Gulf of Aqaba, Kos,
or the temple at Luxor?

A woman I know keeps a pair
of Baskin-Robbins spoons
by the box on the étagère. Some

of her husband is always scoop-
ready to fly (Ziploc-ed)
to places he'd planned to see:

so far, he's in Galway Bay, Bangkok,
Venice, plus Plainview, New Jersey.
For veterans, lots of welcoming

crypts and plots are nearby.
I had your discharge handy,
but it didn't seem right, since

from your island war, only Minnie
the cat was saved, and all
the rest washed out on forgetful

tides. After weeks of banging
a toe at my desk, I went
to the drop at the garden's edge

where we push raked leaves.
I poured slow, yet still
a particle-cloud flew up

and made me cough. The taste
was bitter. When covering leaves
refused to settle, I gave

the heap a kick and nearly
fell off. No neighbor leaning
out for a smoke (I hoped)

was witnessing my—what,
my act of indecent disposal?
In the end, are all choices

bitter, the stubborn body
so loath to yield? What effort
it takes us sad synecdochists

to imagine not ash but flame:
the jagged blossoming, red peaks,
hot gold, my heart annealed.

MEN MOWING
for my father

On my late July drive to you, I can't escape
men mowing. Faced with the season's riot
of vines and weeds, such variety of grasses,
we've exhausted our vocabulary.
We say "green," we say "abundant,"
but we're well beyond knowing how to praise.
At this breakneck pace, we'll be lost,
matchbox toys forgotten on the lawn, sunk
beneath the vegetable ocean of existence.

The essential and pragmatic response is: mowing,
by any and all means. Let the weed whackers
whine, tractor mowers roll at the stately pace
of howdah-bearing elephants. Let old-fashioned
push mowers grudgingly revolve their rusted blades.
It's simple in midsummer, when there are just two
kinds of busy. Your season is simple, too—birds flown,
blinds drawn. Neither growing nor mowing.

The Esperantists

With the last of their funds, they have rented
The Old Masonic Ballroom for Candor's coming out.

The klezmer trio (playing for drinks) strikes up:
here she is in the wide, gilt-framed doorway!

As her escorts pluck at her puffed brocade sleeves,
she steps from the stiff, dazzling cocoon at her feet

and paces unhurried the length of the parquet floor.
From unpainted lips she lets fall recipes, lullabies,

snatches of doo-wop, diagnoses, clear-voiced creeds,
also weather reports. Each Esperantist crowding

around her catches an utterance, mutters it over
by heart. But Candor never stops moving, looks

neither left nor right, and heads for the French doors.
The flock of susurrant Esperantists follows,

abstracted, a buzzing cloud, until it collides
with a noise from out there of children playing.

All ears, the Esperantists jam through the doors,
but outside, no children, no Candor, nothing

except a neglected scrap of garden: hydrangeas,
catmint, spiderwort drooping in the summer sun

under the full weight of shining, the brown
astilbe crackle-leafed, heaps of shade-loving lamium,

papery-dead. Now the sinking sun,
screened by buildings and trees, permits a breeze

to touch the cheeks of the puzzled Esperantists.
The murmurous hum of recitations subsides

or is dissolved into action. Some trace
the garden hose to the tap, some prop leggy stalks

with found twigs, others finger warm earth
for resistless roots and pull. What are the hopeful

sounds of the common life? Glib and raucous,
a mob of crows vacates the tree-tops; passing

geese take their monoglot chorus with them.
For wide light, the open leaves return

unheard thanks, as breast to beloved lip
gives back silence. Undisturbed, the air

erases the pressure shaping tongues have stirred.
What was candor but a name?

No Pear Tree,

but a downpour of blossoms,
white delicate petals drifting
on hair and breast and feet
inexhaustible.
The strange thing was
that I didn't think

> no more than a child
> who wakes to the cold at winter midnight,
> pads in hope to the window and finds
> happiness
> thick in the lamplight's cone,
> snowfall like starlight descending
> ghosting pavement and grass

the strange thing was
I didn't think of summer. I did
not wish for fruit.

DEATH OF AN OLD PROFESSOR DURING PANDEMIC

He was twice-married, once to a woman
and once to a man, his life imitating the art of
    his book about the knight whose never-

    splintering magic lance made him invincible,
and who was revealed as a girl when, doffing
    his visored helmet, her curtain of

    blond hair unfurled to the floor. The day
he died, I went to a poetry reading on Zoom.
    The poets flashed up on my screen, each crowned

    with the same laurel wreath of small boxes,
listening faces in mute(d) chorus. One loss
    in a time of losses. One zero multiplies the obvious

    without unpacking the riddle. I heard
poems of strange incident and odd fact.
    The dead shark on the subway, the reason dogs

    drag their haunches around in circles before
relieving themselves. From neat rows of gleaming
    jars, I tasted grudges home-canned,

    pressure-cooked, griefs brined in old tears.
Did he resolve the mystery, drawing a line
    under the sum of his years? I was ready

    to leap into wonder, but the splash was puddle-deep.
Give me oceans. I want cliff-falls, and croppings
    above the waves, holdfasts for the cobalt

    slap and swell, clutch of kelp
or sea wrack, skitter of foam like a magic
    glass of fractured perspective, each onward

collapsing wave—belated triumph, new-loved loss—
like wet, folded wings cracking a chrysalis
or Monroe's green silk dress slipping to the floor.

Parentalia

Not that I *would* leave flowers at your grave—
supposing the rules allowed it—

when you can't smell or see them.
You didn't drink wine, and milk

is for the cats you never liked. I wish
you were a hungry ghost

who won't stay dead. Demand me something:
I haven't wholly lost

the power of giving. Being bereft of being
loved by you is ruin. Worse,

if *to* love weren't always in the gift of the living.

HELICAL

for Stuart Kessler

As priesthoods probe the genome's mysteries,
unpick the alphabet knitted in chains
of peptides, amino acids, chemical twists
of inert stuff that live, not much remains
to thwart our vanquishing the albatross,
yet here's a figure good to contemplate:
the helix, proof that cross and double-cross
got in on our ground floor, that love and hate
are kissing cousins. Which in turn explains
why the human race can't keep its own hands
off its own throat, and why against the grain's
our route of choice. Only our corkscrew strands
clasp strange familiars. Parallels can't veer,
noble, endless, loneliest when most near.

House Music

In a too-small room in a too-small house
you played Mozart and ragtime for relief.
Man, woman, child, fish, gecko, mouse:
everyone armored in scales and teeth.

You played Mozart and ragtime; for relief,
I sang lieder and "Songs from the Hearth."
Everyone's armor—scales and teeth,
action figures—squeaked and barked

as I sang lieder and "Songs from the Hearth"
out of time, lost my place and cursed my mistakes.
Action figures that squeaked and barked
concealed the slither of black-tongued snakes

a long time. Lost in place, I cursed my mistakes,
discords reverberating. You frowned.
Concealed, the slither of black-tongued snakes
pumped faster, racing round and round

the chords, reverberating when you frowned.
Our two bruised hearts, two thirsty beasts,
pumped faster, racing round the brown
and shrinking wellspring—too used,

our too-bruised hearts, to thirst. The beasts
were weeping, wild-eyed. Still you played,
unshrinking, till the wellspring loosed
bright music, and the creatures stayed

their weeping, mild-eyed while you played:
man, woman, child, fish, gecko, mouse,
bright music of all creatures strayed
in a too-small room in a too-small house.

Two Orioles

Bird of brightest yellow:

lend your leaden namesake
trailing across my page
some of your flash
                        and daring.

            Give wings. Give
                        a pitch in air.

SHOULDERS

I didn't mean to loop that taut line
in a sloppy coil of garter snake surprise.
Its signal-seeking tongue flickered carmine
impotence and filed my admiration under: NOISE.
So I shouldn't have expected it to be basking there
when I turned back. It wasn't. Slither and glide
had foiled my interrogatory stare.
Now I wonder if life-forms can be classified
into two sorts: with shoulders and without.
Over the shoulders means the backward look,
revisions…fictive certainty, invented doubt…
self-ambush…mess. But no shoulders, no crook
in place or time. If I could look behind
by curving ahead, let my opposites meet
and squelch my self-division, I might not mind
crawling where I have to go: who needs feet?
Though I am grateful they've so often brought
me to this green surround, to these befalls,
the creatureliness of creatures beyond thought,
a billion coded patterns: flights or brawls,
freezes, frenzies, covert and in plain sight.
You can breathe on this rise. But I love some,
knotted in on these trails so tight,
that when I walk, the thought of what's to come
floods in and chokes me—subtractions hacking the bruised
landscape. Then before I have the right,
I mourn—as if I could control the ending
with prepaid grief. I feel ashamed, when light
pours thoughtlessly and large. A hawk's shrill
whistle said, what will be is let fall.
It seemed my cue to turn and look, and circle
what I saw: above was the moon's disc, small
and chalky but hooped in unembittered blue;
brittle gold leaves and leaves still branching green;
stumps that flaunted turkey tails; and (what drew
me more) the chance unveilings, now unseen:

last spring's tanager, the neck of the stream
churning a furious froth, the empty spot
the snake, by disappearing, had made gleam
with the plenitude of absence. To loose a knot
or tie it takes the same turning and returning
of the thread, give or take a smart tug.
Which was it now, air and earth both burning
in brilliant dispossession? I could only shrug.

GALLOP

If wishes were horses
We would all ride,
Baby and beggar, remorseless,
Full-fisted with pride.

(All galloping, galloping)

If furies were blackberries
No stone would bide,
But steeples find spurs in their hurry,
All hazards tongue-tied.

(All galloping, galloping)

If hammer were hint, or
Taffeta trump,
The indigo apes of winter
Who harry and scrimp

(All galloping, galloping)

Would rain us quick fishes
Gold in the sluice,
Fling hawks to our wishes
And croon us to roost.

(None galloping, galloping)

Poor Dolly

Gonna dance with the dolly with the hole in her stockin'...

Muted.
Foiled. Not the blood
Moon's thrilling song.
A thimbleful upon a broken
Stem. Wrong. Thirst-
Thin, askew, accursed.
No ping. Unheard.
Spoiled. Stale and gray
Word, blotted and blurred
Spoonful of fluff
Decomposing
In the dirty
Box of day.

A look, then, in lieu
Of a listen. But
The titivated coil
Of you! Frippery
Bedizening fuss,
Pleats and swirls,
Soiled, spotted lace. Dolly,
Only the hole in your
Stocking is honest. Repair
To the plush snuggery, wipe
Your face. The dirty world's
A snare, but worth a dance,
And wanting's no disgrace.

Spring Cold

March snow blooms the bare trees with white
   theoretical blossoms
but fails to sugar-coat the human streets.

   In my sickroom
I'm having it both ways: Kleenex clumps
   of snow, Kleenex

cherry blossoms preposterously in flower.
   This is the cusp
between inhale and exhale, bouncing

   molecules caged
for a split second of poise, brief recess
   from the school

of hard knocks. It's equinoctial March,
   when eggs
stand on end in perfect balance,

   porcelained suns
at ease with the ghosts of chicken past
   and chicken future.

This is the imagination's soft spill
   into the slick
trafficked streets, smooth circuit fused,

   self-sustaining,
unscrambled. The hot pulse slows,
   sweatered,

ears thrum and whine with the beat
   of the body
alone, a solipsist's glory, while

all along the river,
the muddy suck and sigh and settling
of riparian rot

are suspended, the infernal racket
of the blind ferryman's
collisions muffled, logjams resolved.

The Alterations

.... Love is not love
Which alters when it alteration finds...

It's happened so often we think
we're braced for the lurch,
the wound. The woods were

full of ferns, a green clutter.
I sulked, wanting wildflowers,
not this glut. Unwilled,

the scene revolved. Lights by
degrees brightened to an emphatic
gold. On the ground, ferns

in giant sprays were becoming
their own ghosts, sliding
between worlds. My eyes

were fixed on the treetops,
the expected spectacle
of denuding brilliance. Then

calamitous winter,
azure glaciers calving
off, the jungles up

in smoke, ourselves hard
to recognize. Dear love,
no fixed mark prevails,

and even intransigence is
transient. Sapless and pale,
the ferns went modestly,

un-operatically to ground,
nothing to despise. Our
alterations are subtractions

no raging star can possibly
restore. The stage is getting bare.
It's time to improvise.

THE ANDROMEDA

How far can the trunk lean without uprooting?
  That depends where one's sweet-and-low desires lead.

Now that you've struck deep, what's the hold-fast footing
  Worth? A dance? It's a nice calculus of need.

Once a single sun shone, and your saluting
  Simply was enough for trunk and limbs to feed,

Till a sudden growth spurt had you wildly shooting
  Green arabesques each way in air. Any weed

Or hedge provokes you to oblique recruiting
  Of the white and kindly blaze that now you read

Kaleidoscopically in your self-deluding.
  Such shadow-play will, given time, recede.

After the summer's fling, with its mad fruiting,
  You come back to the rock. Sober thoughts concede

Perseus may not turn up. As winter's denuding
  Concentrates and realigns the sun, you need

Only this dry touch, as of midsummer footing
  Heard far off. Night holds you cradled and belee'd

For now, with all your leanings summed up, brooding.

HANDEL IN A TIME OF DISCORD

hearing "As Steals the Morn" played by Voices of Music

As if one more act of aimless
          violence could cure a world
whose malady was aimless violence.
          Or one more shrapneled utterance
                    do anything but maim and sever.

If we can't have silence, then music,
          in a pale rococo room of pearled light.
                    Bowed viols, like bees
rubbing pollen-powdered legs,
          win sweetness from friction,

                    honey from buzzing wood;
the heavy bassoon lets fall
          its rope of golden chequins on two plush
                    and silken voices, singers
who marry lines parting and twining

          and parting again; and the white-bearded
                    oboist tranced, swaying, shoulders
dancing, a wordless prophet. I will make
          his prayer ours: jagged as
                    we are, that such harmony mend

and amend us; its light airs raise
          and revive what lies sunken, dark, or numb;
                    such cordage bind us
to each other's hunger.
          If no such music, then silence.

Note: The first three lines are quoted from Garrett Mattingly, *The Defeat of the Spanish Armada.*

Farming Byzantium

...when we shall be willing to sow the sun and the moon for seeds.
Ralph Waldo Emerson

At the Transcendental Agriculture School
their Singing Masters
taught them to breathe: Asterisms
hyphenated the Continents.
They became Breath:
Persepolises spangled the Aether.
Pearl and Fire
made the furrowed Darkness fertile.

Thus much the Starscript.

A crow's eye gleams
between the rows of
transcendental harvest.
Bound for splendor,
sheaves nod to the stubbled ground,
homesick already.

SOVEREIGN GREEN

The cat's tongue of solitude has its rough consolations.

Green made greener by a borrowed blue.
The fresh waves coming on and on in rows
like Ziegfeld girls.

Now the well-managed horses no longer draw
in their swift footing the gold and pearl chariot.
The diamond axles have stopped revolving.

The noble charioteer is bracketed now
by blue absorption, blue reflection,
above this sovereign green.

After the kingfisher's emerald fury,
the dazzling interchange of air
and water. As if the first principle were

Become something else.

LINES FOR WALKING WEST

Bread on the table and someone to eat it with

   You have your portion

The key in your pocket will not unlock most doors

   Being at home

Sightless in earth or in the water of a green glass jar

   Which is my portion?

A fingertip memorandum in scabs and scars

   Of being at home

Hautboys under the stage, muted trumpets aloft

   Portents of wondrous proportion

The audacious songbirds who braved an approach

   Already at home

In the emporium of abandonment

   We purchased our portion

Shoes with good soles and a spare pair

   All the ways home

Nights westering toward their lockdown

   Splendor their portion
   Wine-blue home

Transit of Venus

Your name is the badge of every absence,
a hole in the sun, beloved silence,

globed darkness like a lavalier.
What is it worth, the singular?
One great blue heron where we saw a pair,

cormorant among a mob of crows.
A rich thing is exalted by shadows,

each bead of shattered mercury a star.
Darkness neighbors you and tugs you clear,

beggar-king love, fugitive sense.
Your name is the badge of every absence.

Cormorant among a mob of crows,
I'm strange to myself in the shadows,
more strange in light that neither slows

nor speeds the stain across its blaze.
In your name I wait.

The Gift

New Year's Day and the big reeds bowing over the stream's headlong,
white churn, only one back-flowing current glazing and glazing a black
smooth stone, and you said *This year it will be fifty years.* Fuck years.
Fuck tick, fuck tock, first and thirty-first, clepsydra, clock, calendar,
sunfuckingdial, tolling spire. Fuck my egg-timing hourglass: reversible liar!
I blame the Babylonian who set a collar in the sky, twelve emblems
nailed with stars, endless ouroboros, when time's really a worm draggling
out its days. I don't want a ring or a bracelet. No circles. Not a glimmer
of eternity. You know what I want, love: only a next day, and a next.
Like you I just want more.

Collateral Beauty

Nothing in nature is a metaphor.
Everything is.
                Stephen Dunn, "The Past"

Let's talk about the imperatives of damaged things.
We were lopping away at a bunch of grotesque invasive grass
when the hibiscus, in ill-starred proximity to the intended clump,
got chopped. Curtains, we thought.
But a few weeks later it gamely bore
on one spindly, remnant stem more buds
than we could have dreamed.
The scuttled present is big with futures, un-gainsayable.
Against all odds, they bloomed, six dolly-faced flowers
Pepto-Bismol pink, the size of dinner plates.
I'm in love, but that proves nothing.
My darlings' ends are light-years removed
from my doting pride.
Here's another thing: sunset confuses me,
luxuriant dying that spreads like spilled paint
across night's visibly deepening design
and quickens the zenith with a frolicsome bestiary
doomed to the insatiable dark.
Yet a mere twelve hours later, in the pale
wash of morning, it's business as usual.
The kid next door saws away and fingers the frets;
traffic hums the tritone; the jay resumes its indignation.
I swear, only the daily-ness of it
keeps me from a continual cold sweat:
the world, the world is a dreadful place.
My naked senses go ricocheting and pinballing
around the dings and flashes of the biomass,
a landscape of covert urgencies without number.
What hope for someone who thinks all the world's a page?
(And don't tell me thinking helps:
it's buff from sparring with the greats,
but it reeks of the gym.) In all this terror and glory,
I supplicate you on the margins, ceaseless ones.

I *am* yours; let me belong to you
by whom I am clothed and companioned until I cease.
I clasp your non-existent knees,
you powers innocent of augury. You whose gift it is
to be deaf to songs of elegy as of wonder.

Acknowledgments

I am very grateful to the publications in which the following poems first appeared. A special thank you to Pauline Watts for sharing with me her beautiful photographs, three of which directly inspired "Two Ravens," "Persimmons on the Ground," and "White Bird / Bare Tree."

Alabama Literary Review: "Spring Cold"
American Journal of Poetry: "Contradance"; "Progress"
Angle: "House Music"
Common Ground Review: "Interrogatories"
Crosswinds: "The Old Couple"
The Cumberland River Review: "Dime Saint, Nickel Devil"; "About the Ponies"; "The Amaryllis"; "The Difference"; "Children Playing (Nones)"; "Tyranny (II)"
Dark Wood: "Transit of Venus"
Descant: "The Parlor Wit"
Front Range Review: "Imago"
The Georgia Review: "Girl Reading the *Aeneid* on the Subway"
Glimpse: "Tyranny (I)"
Lightwood: "Was It Bashō"; "White Bird / Bare Tree"; "Touch Wood (Compline)"
Lumina: "Persimmons on the Ground"; "No Pear Tree," (as "Fruit")
Michigan Quarterly Review: "Men Mowing"; "Parentalia"
Plant-Human Quarterly: "Profit"
Salamander: "The Gift"
The Same: "Helical"
Slant: "Noon (Sext)"
Southern Poetry Review: "Scene, With Supporting Cast of Facts"; "Backyard (Tierce)"
Spillway: "Baby Mantis"; "Two Orioles"; "Poor Dolly"
Valley Voices: "Principles"; "Heat Wave"; "Farming Byzantium"

"Girl Reading the *Aeneid* on the Subway" also appeared on Poetry Daily.
"The Amaryllis" was anthologized in *The Cumberland River Review: The First Five Years*

Heartfelt thanks to Susana Case, Penny Freeland, Kate Johnson, Bern Mulvey, and Margo Stever for their insight and generosity; to Larry Moore and Sheila Potter of Broadstone Books for their editorial wisdom and kindness.

About the Author

Ann Lauinger's previous books of poetry are *Persuasions of Fall* (University of Utah, 2004), winner of the Agha Shahid Ali Prize in Poetry, and *Against Butterflies* (Little Red Tree Publishing, 2013). Her poems have appeared in publications from *Alimentum* to *Zone 3*, including *The Cumberland River Review*, *Georgia Review*, *Lightwood*, *Michigan Quarterly Review*, *Parnassus*, *The Same*, *Smartish Pace*, and *The Southern Poetry Review*. Translations have appeared in *Levania*, *The Massachusetts Review*, and *Transference*. Her work has been included in anthologies such as *The Bedford Introduction to Literature*, *Decomposition*, and *In a Fine Frenzy: Poets Respond to Shakespeare* and been featured on Poetry Daily, Verse Daily, and Martha Stewart Living Radio. Professor Emerita of Literature at Sarah Lawrence College, she is a member of the Slapering Hol Press Advisory Committee and lives in Ossining, New York.